AF225771

Published by UTU Media® - © 2026 Bridget Irby
No part of this book may be reproduced or transmitted in any form or by any means, electronic or mechanical, including photocopying and recording, or by information storage or retrieval system, except as may be expressly permitted in writing by the publisher.
ISBN - 9781966130017
Unless indicated otherwise, all Scriptures marked KJV are taken from the KING JAMES VERSION (KJV): KING JAMES VERSION, public domain.
Printed in the United States of America

Dear Reader,
This Book Is Dedicated To You.

Your journey may not always be easy but, it is worth it.
I pray you find the words inside helpful and healing.

Dear Friend,

Have you ever felt it? That gentle whisper in your heart telling you that God has so much more for your life? That there's a deeper relationship with Him waiting just around the corner, if only you knew how to get there?

Maybe you're doing all the "right" things. You're reading your Bible (or at least trying to), showing up to church (most Sundays), and praying (even if sometimes it feels like your prayers are hitting the ceiling and bouncing right back). Yet somehow, it feels like you're stuck in spiritual quicksand – the more you struggle, the deeper you sink.

Here's the truth: Sometimes, the path to more of God isn't about doing more things right – **it's about stopping the things that are holding you back**.

This is exactly why I created the "You Are Not Called" series. These books aren't about adding more to your spiritual to-do list. Instead, they're about gaining freedom by doing less – freedom from anxiety that steals your peace, freedom from fear that holds you captive, freedom from anger that robs your joy, freedom from shame that keeps you hidden, and freedom from loneliness that makes you feel disconnected from God and others.

I'm not writing these books from some lofty spiritual mountaintop. I'm writing as someone who has crawled through the valleys of anxiety, fear, anger, shame, and loneliness – and discovered that God was there all along, waiting to show me a better way. As an ordained minister, yes, but more importantly, as a woman who has lived every word on these pages, I can tell you with absolute certainty: You are not called to live this way. You are not called to be anxious, afraid, angry, ashamed, or alone. These struggles are not your inheritance as a child of God.

Think of this series as your spiritual "stop it" list. Just like a gardener needs to pull out weeds before planting new seeds, we need to identify and remove the things that are choking our spiritual growth.

I've seen God's transformative power firsthand. Each book in this series represents a battle I've fought and won, not through my own strength, but through discovering what God says about who we are and what we're called to be.

This journey won't always be easy but I promise you this: if you're ready to let go of what's holding you back, if you're willing to challenge the lies you've believed, and if you're prepared to step into the freedom God has for you, your life will never be the same. Because the truth is, sister, you were created for more than just surviving – you were created to thrive.

With faith, hope, and a whole lot of grace,

Bridget

xoxo

Christian Friends Are The Best Friends!

Hey Friend,

Before we dive into this journey of overcoming anxiety, I want to extend a special invitation to you. An invitation to not just read this book, but to truly live out its principles alongside other powerful Christian women.

You and I both know, we weren't meant to walk this path alone.

As Ecclesiastes 4:12 reminds us, "Though one may be overpowered, two can defend themselves. A cord of three strands is not quickly broken." This wisdom isn't just for ancient times - it's for us, right here, right now.

That's why I want to invite you to do life with me and other women just like you inside The Sisterhood. If you don't already have a strong support group of sound-minded, Christ-led sisters who inspire, uplift, and challenge you to live out your highest life, this is for you.

The Sisterhood is more than just a community - it's a place where we do life together. It's where we laugh, cry, pray, and grow side by side. It's where we put into practice the very principles you'll be reading about in this book.

Imagine having a group of sisters who:
- Pray, cry, and laugh with you through all of life's twists and turns
- Celebrate with you as you deepen your relationship with Christ
- Offer wise counsel to you when life gets complicated
- Stand with you in prayer as you pursue your God-given calling

This is what we do in The Sisterhood. Together, we're building the village that we all need. Just visit www.missiondrivensisters.com to join.

Remember, you weren't meant to do this alone. Let's link arms and become that unbreakable three-strand cord together!

Lots of love,

Bridget

xoxo

Since you're holding this book, I want you to hear my heart clearly: **I wrote this study because I've lived this battle.**

I've prayed prayers through tears.

I've whispered Scripture while panic tried to take my breath.

I've asked God why anxiety felt louder than His promises at times.

And I've experienced His healing, His comfort, and His peace in the places I once thought were too overwhelmed to repair.

This study isn't written from a distance — it's written from the middle of my own journey with God, from the days He strengthened me when I felt weak, and from the countless moments He reminded me: *"You are not called to be anxious — you are called to trust Me."*

I've watched God heal the deepest parts of me through Scripture, through community, through honesty, and through His presence. And I believe with everything in me that He can do the same for you.

Take your time with these pages. Breathe. Let God meet you. Don't rush the process — peace grows steadily, not suddenly.

Thank you for trusting me to walk with you. I'm honored to stand beside you in this healing.

Love you,
Bridget

Free Resources

Hey there, superstar!

I'm so proud of you for starting this journey and because I'm not about to send you out there empty-handed, I've got some awesome resources to help you on your journey.

Think of these as your toolkit. They're like the Swiss Army knife of emotional and spiritual growth - versatile, handy, and they might just save you in a pinch (though maybe don't try to use them to open a can or cut down a small tree).

To access the resources,
simply visit
www.youarenotcalled.com.

Inside, you'll have to the above
resources plus much more!

A Not-So-Boring-But-Very-Important Disclaimer

(Please Read This, Even If You Usually Skip These Things)

Before we dive into this adventure together, we need to have a little chat. You know, the kind that usually comes with a cup of coffee and a "Now, don't freak out, but..." opener. So, grab your beverage of choice (I won't judge if it's not coffee), and let's get real for a moment.

First things first: I am not a doctor, therapist, counselor, or any other type of licensed mental health professional. I know, shocking right? Despite my incredible ability to dispense wisdom and wit (if I do say so myself), my qualifications are more in the realm of "life experience" and "passionate Jesus follower" than "Ph.D. in Psychology."

This book, as awesome as it is (and trust me, it's pretty awesome), is not meant to replace the invaluable work of trained professionals. Think of it more as a heart-to-heart with a friend who's been there, done that, and got the t-shirt (and maybe a few therapy sessions) to prove it.

If you're dealing with severe anger issues, depression, anxiety, or any other mental health concerns, **please, please, PLEASE seek help from a qualified professional.** They have tools in their toolbox that go way beyond what I can offer here. *(Plus, they probably have comfier couches for you to sit on while you talk.)*

This book is meant to be a companion on your journey, not your only guide. It's like having a workout buddy – super helpful and motivating, but not a substitute for a trained physical therapist if you've got a serious injury.

So, if at any point while reading this book you think, "Wow, I could really use some professional help with this," then congratulations! You've just had an incredibly mature and self-aware moment. Seriously, give yourself a pat on the back, then go find yourself a therapist. Your future self will thank you.

Remember, seeking help is not a sign of weakness. It's a sign that you're brave enough to admit you don't have all the answers (welcome to the club, by the way) and smart enough to ask for guidance. That's the kind of wisdom that would make Solomon proud!

Now, with all that said, I truly believe that this book has the potential to be a powerful tool in your spiritual and emotional growth journey. Just think of it as one piece of your "becoming-the-best-version-of-yourself" puzzle, not the whole picture.

So, are we clear? This book = awesome friend and spiritual cheerleader. Trained professionals = necessary allies for serious stuff. You = amazing child of God who deserves all the help and support you can get.

Alright, now that we've got that out of the way, let's get back to the good stuff. You've got a life-changing journey ahead of you, and I, for one, can't wait to see where it takes you. Just remember, if the road gets too bumpy, don't be afraid to call in some professional reinforcements. After all, even Batman needed Alfred, right?

Remember...

There's no rush.

You and me, love, we've got our whole lives to figure this thing out. Don't let rushing steal your joy.

There's no wrong answer.

This is unique to you and you simply cannot get it wrong. Just be honest with yourself and we can go from there.

You are doing great.

High five sister! Just the fact that you are here, with God, working on you says everything. Congratulations!

Introduction

Anxiety is one of the most silent battles in the Christian walk. It hides behind busy schedules, forced smiles, perfectly curated social media posts, and "I'm fine" replies that keep others out while fear rages within.

So many daughters of God love Jesus deeply but are quietly drowning in thoughts they can't control, emotions they can't explain, and pressure they can't seem to shake.

For years, the Church has unintentionally taught us to deal with anxiety by "being stronger," "praying harder," or "having more faith." And while prayer and faith are essential, they were never meant to replace the deeper emotional, physical, and spiritual healing God wants to do in us.

That's why this study exists — not to shame you, silence your struggle, or give you spiritual clichés, but to guide you gently back to the truth: *you are not called to be anxious.*

You are called and created to live in God's peace, walk in His confidence, and experience His presence in every part of your life.

Through these nine weeks, you will learn how anxiety affects your body, your thoughts, your relationships, your pace, your decisions, and your connection with God.

You will discover practical tools and biblical truth woven together in a way that meets you exactly where you are. You won't be rushed or criticized — you'll be guided, supported, and strengthened.

This study is not about achieving "perfect calm."

It's about learning to recognize God's voice over anxiety's voice. It's about healing the parts of you that fear tried to shape. It's about becoming a woman who doesn't bow to anxious thoughts but rises above them with wisdom, discernment, and Holy Spirit power.

My prayer is that these pages feel like a safe place — a place where you can breathe again, a place where you feel seen, a place where you remember that God is not disappointed in you. He is with you. He is working in you. And He is leading you into a life where peace is possible, sustainable, and powerful.

Welcome to your journey back to peace.

You're not behind.

You're not broken.

You're right on time.

Week One

Anxiety rarely announces itself with a bang. Anxiety doesn't usually begin as panic.

It begins as a whisper. A soft nudge. A little tightening in your chest or a quickened heartbeat you brush off because "that's just life."

And before you know it, that whisper grows louder. That nudge becomes a shove. Your mind starts sprinting toward every worst-case scenario it can imagine, and suddenly you're living like something bad is always about to happen.

Sis, anxiety is a thief. *And a skilled one.*

It doesn't break down your door—it slides in through the cracks.

The enemy knows he doesn't need to destroy you to stop you. *He just needs to distract you.* If he can keep your thoughts running wild, he can keep your spirit tired, your faith shaky, and your peace nonexistent.

Anxiety is one of his quietest—and most effective—strategies.

But here's the truth: you were not meant to live on high alert. You were never created to carry the emotional load you've been dragging behind you. God didn't call you to survive your life—He called you to live it <u>abundantly</u>.

Anxiety is not abundance.

Anxiety is a thief.

Jesus told us the enemy's plan plainly: to steal, kill, and destroy. If you've lost peace—if joy feels out of reach, if rest feels impossible—that's not "just how you are." That's evidence of a battle you were never meant to fight alone.

Today, pause and acknowledge the places anxiety has been stealing from you.

Awareness is not weakness—it's the first step toward reclaiming what's yours.

Take some time now to read and pray over today's scripture: **John 10:10.**

Bible Reading

READ JOHN 10:10 (KJV)

Spend time praying right now that God reveal to you where the enemy is attacking your mind.

Journal your thoughts below. Identify which of your worries are real and which are just created to distract you from your purpose and calling.

Today's Challenge

Write down at least one thing anxiety convinces you to worry about daily.

Ask yourself if this is a valid worry or a lie from the enemy.

If not, then write God's truth beside it.

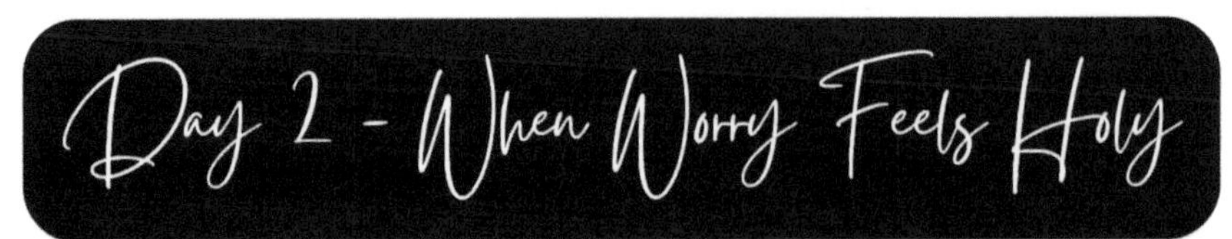

Let's be honest—some of us have treated worry like it's part of being a "good Christian woman."

We've confused *anxiety* with *responsibility*. We've labeled *overthinking* as being *prepared*. We've mistaken carrying everyone's burdens as being **caring**.

Somewhere along the line, worry started to feel... *holy*.

You tell yourself, *"If I don't think about it, who will?"* Sis, **God will**. That's literally His job description.

A lot of Christian women carry anxiety because they've been taught (directly or indirectly) that peace is passive, but worry is **proof you care**.

But Scripture never commands you to stay awake all night replaying conversations or imagining disasters. Scripture invites you—*again and again*—to pray, release, and receive peace.

But **peace requires trust.** And trust requires putting control in God's hands - not yours.

Here's the thing, sis, your desperate attempts to control everything and overthink everything and worry about everything are only illusions that give you a sense of control. In reality, the only thing we're actually in control of are our responses and our own actions. That's it, friend. No amount of worry is going to change that.

There was a season where I thought worrying meant I was being responsible. If I thought about the situation from every angle, I convinced myself I was being wise. In reality, I was exhausted, tormented, and spiritually distracted. My "wisdom" was actually fear wearing a church dress.

Paul doesn't say, *"Try not to worry."*

He says, **Do not be anxious about anything.**

And then he tells us how: pray, ask, thank God, and watch peace guard your heart.

Peace is not the reward for controlling everything.

Peace is the fruit of surrendering everything to the only one who has real control.

READ PHILIPPIANS 4:6–7
(KJV)

Read the scripture then spend time in prayer asking God to reveal to you what you need to know to give up the idol of worry in your life.

Answer this question below: Where have you mislabeled worry as wisdom, responsibility, or preparation?

Give God one thing today you've been holding onto. Pray, release it, and refuse to take it back. Use the space below to record your prayer.

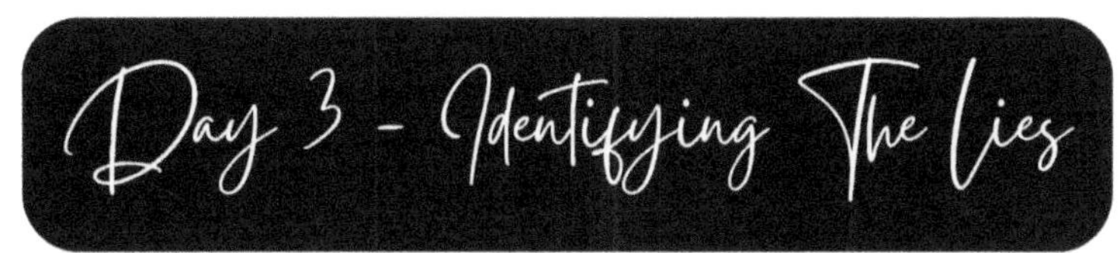

Anxiety has a script. And if we're not paying attention, we start repeating its lines like they're truth. The enemy loves to whisper lies like:

- *"You're not safe."*

- *"You're not enough."*

- *"Something bad is coming."*

- *"You can't handle what's next."*

Sound familiar?

Anxiety always begins with a lie—one that goes unchallenged long enough to feel true. But Scripture gives us a strategy: **take every thought captive and make it obedient to Christ.**

That means you get to interrogate your thoughts before letting them live in your mind. That's right, sis. Not every thought you have is true. Not every thought you have is real. Not every thought you have is serving you.

Imagine your thoughts lined up at the door of your mind like they're trying to enter a secured building. *Your job isn't to let everyone in.* **Your job is security.**

Ask every anxious thought, *"Who sent you?"* **If it didn't come from God, it doesn't get access.**

Today we're exposing the lies anxiety has been feeding you.

- Lie: *"I'm alone in this."*
  - Truth: God is with me AND God sends people to walk with me.
- Lie: *"I have to figure everything out."*
  - Truth: God directs my steps.
- Lie: *"I'm not strong enough."*
  - Truth: His strength is made perfect in my weakness.
- Lie: *"I'll never have peace."*
  - Truth: Peace is my inheritance and right as a child of God. The enemy wants to steal it but I am stronger than my thoughts.

It's time to stop rehearsing fear and start replacing it with truth.

READ 2 CORINTHIANS 10:5 (KJV)

What does it mean to you to take every thought captive? Are your thoughts obedient to and congruent with the heart of Christ? Take some time to pray over this scripture with a heart that seeks God's will and clarity. Journal your thoughts and answers below.

Identify what thoughts you have that are causing worry and anxiety. Question the thought to uncover if it is true or a lie. Ask yourself: *Do you have any control over the outcome? Will worrying or having anxiety about this issue help the situation? What will help the situation?* Then define actions that will actually help the situation.

Thought	Lie or Truth?	Action Moving Forward

Anxiety loves to take a single thought and spin it into a catastrophic movie no one asked to watch.

One moment you're living your life, and the next your mind has sprinted twelve steps into the future imagining every possible disaster.

It's exhausting. It's unproductive. And Jesus says it doesn't add one hour to your life.

Here's the truth: *anxiety turns thoughts into enemies.*

And half the time, your own mind becomes the loudest critic in the room.

If your brain were a toddler, anxiety is the moment it throws itself onto the floor screaming over something that hasn't even happened yet.

And you're standing there like, *"Really? THIS is what we're doing today?"*

But here's the good news: **you're the parent in this metaphor.**

You get to decide what behavior gets attention. You can't always control the first thought—*but you absolutely can control the second.*

When anxious thoughts show up, you have two choices:

Feed the thought through spiraling down negativity road.

or

Redirect the thought and yourself by reminding yourself of the real truth.

Redirecting isn't denial.

It's discipline.

Jesus tells us to shift our focus *from fear to trust, from lack to provision, from spiraling to seeking.*

You need to guide your thoughts the same way you'd guide a child—*firmly, compassionately, and consistently.*

Bible Reading

READ MATTHEW 6:27 (KJV)

What do you think today's reading means in the context of your life? Why was this teaching so important that Jesus shared it during what would be one of his most famous and most preached upon sermons?

Journal your thoughts below after reading and spending time in prayer.

Today, interrupt every anxious thought with one sentence:
"God is with me, and He is in control."

God's peace doesn't just comfort you—*it guards you.*

His peace stands watch over your heart like a divine security detail assigned to protect your mind from intruding thoughts.

That's not poetic exaggeration—that's **Scripture**.

Peace is not passive.

Peace has an agenda: *to keep you safe.*

But peace can only guard **what you actually give over to God.**

- If you're still clutching the problem, *peace can't cover it.*
  - If you're still rehearsing the fear, *peace can't replace it.*
    - If you're still carrying what wasn't meant for you, *peace can't lighten the load.*

Think of peace like standing under an umbrella in a storm. *The storm doesn't disappear because you stepped under it—but you're protected.* You stop being drenched by the fear that used to soak you.

The more you trust God, the more ground peace covers.

Today, imagine peace covering your mind like a blanket—*warm, protective, steadying.*

Imagine peace guarding your thoughts like a shield.

Imagine peace holding back the flood of anxiety that once overwhelmed you.

Listen to me friend - **you are not called to be anxious.**

You are called to be guarded by a peace that only comes from your creator.

READ JOHN 14:27 (KJV)

Spend time reading this scripture and going to God in prayer. Identify where you are seeking peace from this world, from yourself, from those around you, and from every other avenue you attempt to find. Journal your thoughts and revelations below. Be sure to answer the question: What do I need to place under God's peace today?

Pray for God's supernatural peace to guard your heart and mind. Write out your prayer below. Visualize yourself laying your worries at the feet of God as you pray.

Weekly Recap

This week, you peeled back the layers of anxiety to see what's really been happening beneath the surface. You recognized the subtle ways anxiety has *stolen your peace, invaded your thoughts, and shaped your days.*

You identified the lies it whispers and the toll it takes on your spirit. You opened the door for truth to step in and take its rightful place.

Before you rush into the next week, pause.

Breathe.

Reflect.

- *Where did you feel God's presence most clearly this week?*

  - *Which truth stood out to you?*

    - *What thought pattern are you most ready to release?*

Remember: healing doesn't always feel like a single breakthrough moment. Sometimes it's a quiet shift, a new habit, a different choice made consistently.

That's transformation. That's renewal. That's growth.

You're not who you were last week.

You're already changing.

Let God highlight the moments of victory, big and small. Celebrate them. Thank Him for them. Carry those truths forward.

Weekly Challenge

Choose one anxious thought you've battled for years and commit to replacing it daily. Write it on a sticky note or keep it in your phone—somewhere you'll see it often.

Beside it, write the truth God has spoken over you. Every time the anxious thought rises up, speak God's truth out loud. This is spiritual training. This is renewing your mind. This is how you take thoughts captive and make them obedient to Christ. Set a reminder in your phone if you need to.

Make it practical.

Make it consistent.

By the end of this week, you're going to see a shift—not because the problem disappears, but because your mind is beginning to agree with God more than your fear.

Weekly Prayer

Dear Father,

Thank You for showing me that *anxiety is not my identity.*

Reveal to me every lie I've believed and so that I may replace it with Your truth.

Guard my mind with Your peace and steady my heart when fear tries to rise.

Help me recognize Your presence in every moment and trust You with every detail.

I release what I cannot control and choose to rest in Your strength. Lead me into deeper peace this week.

In Jesus' name,
Amen.

Week Two

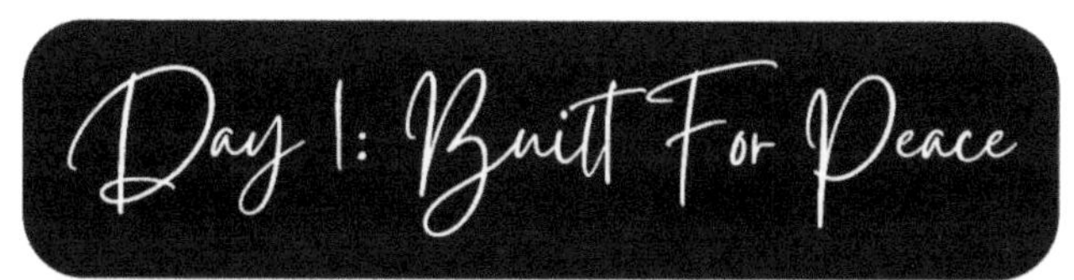

There's a huge difference between being responsible and being weighed down. But most of us were never taught that difference. Instead, we learned to push through, hold it together, and carry everything ourselves because "that's what strong women do."

Listen friend, **God never called you to be strong apart from Him**.

He didn't ask you to drag the weight of your responsibilities, relationships, fears, and future around like a 200-pound backpack. *He asked you to cast your cares — **not collect them.***

This week is about learning to release the things that are weighing you down, even the things you think you "should" be able to handle. God invites you into a lighter way of living — not because the world gets easier, but because He shoulders the weight with you.

Somewhere along the line, many of us made an internal vow: *"If I don't handle it, it won't get done."* So we carry it all — the emotions, the expectations, the pressure, the fears, the outcomes. We carry our family's struggles, our children's choices, our finances, our friend's crises, our trauma, our to-do list, our future... everything. And we wonder why we feel anxious, exhausted, and overwhelmed.

Sis, you weren't designed to carry the weight of the world. *That's God's job.*

1 Peter 5:7 says, *"Cast all your anxiety on Him because He cares for you."* Notice that word: **cast**. Not "consider," not "pray about," not "talk to your friends about." CAST. Throw it off. Release it. Put it on God's side of the line.

God isn't asking you to pretend you're fine. He's asking you to bring Him what you're not meant to hold.

Think of anxiety like a heavy box someone handed you without warning. You pick it up out of habit — because you always pick everything up — but it wasn't meant for you. God is standing there with open hands saying, *"Give it to Me. I can carry this. You can't."*

You don't prove your strength by holding everything.
You prove your faith by releasing what was never yours.

Bible Reading

**READ, REFLECT, & PRAY ON
1 PETER 5:7 (KJV)**

Journal Prompt:

What are you carrying right now that God

never asked you to hold?

Below, write down at least three burdens you've been carrying and pray this:
"Lord, I give You what no longer belongs to me."

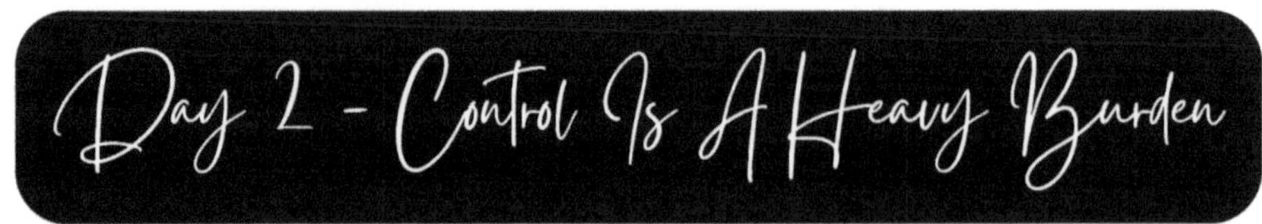

If anxiety had a favorite hiding place, it would be in our desire for control.

That's good, sis. So good, let me say it again: **If anxiety had a favorite hiding place, it would be in our desire for control.** *Our desire to figure everything out. To predict the outcome. To understand everything and everyone. To manage emotions and expectations. To be the best in impossible situations.*

Trying to manage everything and everyone around us feels safe — like we're preventing disaster. But in reality, control is just fear dressed up as responsibility.

We say things like:

- *"If I don't plan for the worst, who will?"*

- *"If I don't prepare for every outcome, we won't be ready."*

- *"If I let go, everything might fall apart."*

But sis… things are falling apart because you're trying to hold what only God can sustain.

Psalm 55:22 says, "Cast your burden on the Lord, and He will sustain you." Not **you** will sustain **you**. He will. God's job is to sustain. **Your job is to surrender.**

That stung, I know. It stings even when I write it. Surrender feels unsafe. It's terrifying. I've been in control for as long as I can remember. What is going to happen if I surrender everything to God? Won't my whole world just fly right off it's axis?

Control feels easier than trust because control gives the illusion that you're in charge of the outcome. Trust requires believing God is good even when you can't predict the next chapter.

Letting go doesn't mean you don't care.

Letting go means you finally believe God can do what you can't.

When you release control, you actually make room for peace.

You make room for God to move.

You make room for answers you never could've strategized.

Bible Reading

READ, REFLECT, & PRAY ON
PSALM 55:22 (KJV)

Journal Prompt:

Where have you been holding on tightly

because it felt safer than trusting God?

Today's Challenge

Choose one situation you've tried to control and say aloud:
"God, I trust Your hands more than my fear."
Below, write out what it will look like to live this out each day.

Jesus didn't say, "Come to Me, all who are pretending they're fine."

He didn't say, "Come to Me, all who are strong enough to keep going."

He said, **"Come to Me, all who are weary and burdened."**

This could also be translated as:
> *Come to Me, you who are overwhelmed.*
>
> *Come to Me, you who are carrying things you've never said out loud.*
>
> *Come to Me, you who smile all day and cry at night.*
>
> *Come to Me, you who feel like you're drowning on the inside while everyone else thinks you're swimming.*

God cares about what you carry because God cares about you.

Anxiety often convinces you that your worries are "too small" or "too much" for God. But Jesus invites you into rest — not because your problems disappear, but because He carries what you cannot.

The Greek word Jesus uses for "burden" references something too heavy for one person to lift. He wasn't asking you to drag your anxiety around with spiritual determination. He was offering to take the weight from your hands.

When you refuse to give God your burdens, you're not being strong — you're being crushed.

When you surrender your burdens, you step into supernatural peace.

Journal Prompt:

What burden do you hesitate to bring to God because you feel like you "should" be able to handle it?

Pray Matthew 11:28 out loud and invite Jesus into the place where you feel the most worn down. Journal your thoughts, experience, and observations below.

Day 4 – Surrender As A Daily Practice

If surrender were easy, you'd only have to do it once. But surrender is not a moment — it's a practice. A rhythm. A posture of the heart that says, *"God, I trust You more than I trust my own understanding."*

Anxiety grows when we cling tightly to our own plans.

Peace grows when we loosen our grip and place our hope in God's wisdom.

Proverbs 3:5–6 is a blueprint for daily surrender:
- Trust in the Lord with all your heart
- Do not lean on your own understanding
- Acknowledge Him in all your ways
- He will make your paths straight

Notice the order — **surrender first,** *clarity second.*

Most of us want clarity before surrender. God says, *"No, daughter. Trust Me. THEN I'll show you the way."*

Every morning, you have a choice: Carry your cares or cast them.

Some days you'll hand your worries to God once. Other days you'll hand Him the same worry fifty times. And that's okay.

The key to surrender is not perfection — it's persistence.

It's choosing to make the choice to surrender to God every single day - even when it's hard, even when you don't understand, even when it's more comfortable to keep your white knuckle grip on everything around you. You can still choose to obey God's command.

Bible Reading

Journal Prompt:

Where do you need clarity, but God is

asking for trust first?

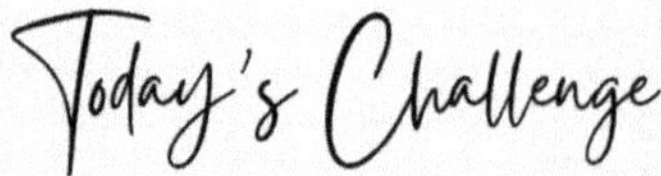

One of the most practical ways to release anxiety is to physically symbolize what you're spiritually surrendering. Today we're creating something simple but powerful: The Care Box.

Here's how it works:

Find a small box, basket, or container. Write the words "CARES GO HERE" on it. Throughout the week, anytime anxiety rises, write the worry on a piece of paper and place it inside the box. This symbolizes casting your cares onto God — not carrying them around in your mind.
This isn't childish. It's biblical.

Philippians 4:6 tells us to turn our worries into prayers and our anxieties into supplications. The Care Box is a physical reminder that you are not meant to hold everything.

When your mind tries to pick the worry back up — because it will — remind yourself: "It's in the box. God has it now."

Over time, you'll begin to feel the difference. The act of releasing your anxiety stops being symbolic and starts becoming spiritual. You'll catch yourself handing things to God faster. You'll feel peace coming sooner. You'll notice you're not living clenched anymore.

What is the first worry you need to place in your Care Box?

Weekly Recap

This week taught you something foundational: you are not responsible for carrying everything. Anxiety grows where you grip life too tightly. Peace grows where you hand it back to God.

As you look back over the past few days, notice where God gently encouraged you to loosen your grasp. Notice where you felt convicted to stop controlling outcomes. Notice where you sensed His presence lifting a burden you barely had words for.

Maybe you felt a shift. Maybe you felt resistance. Maybe surrender felt both beautiful and terrifying.

That's normal.

You're unlearning years of self-reliance and learning a new way of living — a biblical way.

Take time to review the burdens you wrote down earlier this week. Read them again. Then ask yourself honestly: *"Am I still carrying any of these?"*

If the answer is yes — place them in your Care Box today.

If the answer is no — celebrate the peace you're stepping into.

This week was about release.

Next week will be about renewal.

God is drawing you into deeper peace, one surrendered worry at a time.

Weekly Challenge

Every morning this week, choose one burden from your Care Box to intentionally pray over. But here's the key: don't pray anxious prayers. *Pray surrendered ones.*

Instead of "Lord, please fix this," try: "Lord, I trust You with this." Instead of rehearsing the problem, rehearse God's promises.

At the end of each day, evaluate:

- *Did I carry anything today God told me to cast?*
- *Did I try to control something that wasn't mine?*
- *Did I give God room to move?*

If the answer is yes — place it in the box.

Every time you release something, you're building a lifestyle of peace.

Weekly Prayer

Dear Father,

Thank You for caring about every burden I carry.

Teach me to release what was never meant for my hands.

Help me trust that Your strength is greater than my fear, Your wisdom greater than my control, and Your peace greater than my anxiety.

I place my worries into Your care and ask You to guide my steps with clarity and calm.

Make surrender my first instinct, not my last resort.

In Jesus' name,
Amen.

Week Three

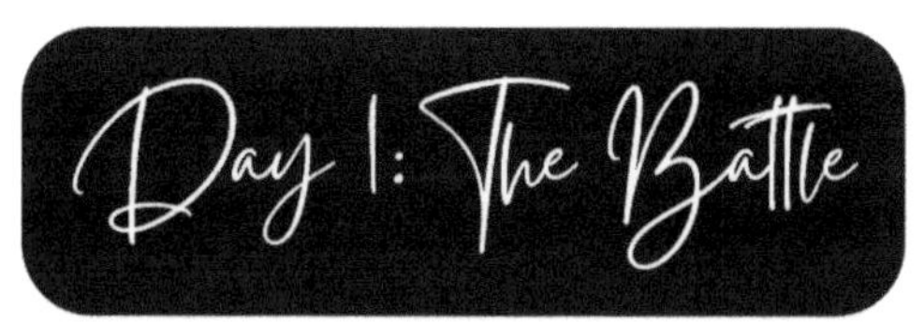

Before anxiety ever shows up in your body, it starts in your thoughts. Every racing heartbeat, every stomach drop, every moment your chest tightens — it all begins with a pattern of thinking the enemy has repeated long enough for you to believe it. But Romans 12:2 tells us *transformation happens when your mind is renewed.*

Not your circumstances. Not your feelings. Your **mind**.

This week isn't about pretending anxious thoughts don't exist. It's about learning to redirect them, interrupt them, and replace them. You're going to learn how to take back control of your thought life, not by trying harder, but by thinking with Heaven's perspective.

Peace isn't the absence of anxious thoughts — it's the authority to rise above them.

If your life feels chaotic, look at your thoughts. If your heart feels anxious, look at your thoughts. If your spirit feels heavy, look at your thoughts.

Why? Because the mind is the battleground where anxiety fights the hardest. Anxiety doesn't start with symptoms — it starts with suggestions. Quiet whispers that build into narratives that build into beliefs.

Your mind is powerful. God designed it that way. But if you're not intentionally renewing your mind with truth, anxiety will happily renew it with fear.

The enemy doesn't need your mind to be destroyed — he just needs it to be distracted, overwhelmed, exhausted, and unfocused. Because a tired mind is an easy target.

But here's the good news: you don't have to live mentally defeated. You get to choose what you think. You get to choose what stays. You get to choose what goes.

Today is about recognizing that your thoughts are not the boss of you. You have the authority — through Christ — to redirect your mind toward truth.

Bible Reading

Journal Prompt:

What thought has been ruling your emotions lately? How can you take control back from this thought?

Write down at least one (more if you can) anxious thought below — then draw a
line through it and write, "This is not truth."

If we're being real, your brain can act like a toddler who drank a Red Bull. It runs, it jumps, it panics, it screams, it imagines disasters, and it has absolutely no regard for peace.

And if you don't train it, it will run your life.

But Scripture says we take thoughts captive.

Not the other way around.

2 Corinthians 10:5 gives you authority to escort every anxious thought out of your mind like an unwelcome guest. You don't have to entertain it. You don't have to negotiate with it. You don't have to sit in fear while it rewrites your reality.

Thought: "I can't handle this."

Truth: "God strengthens me."

Thought: "Something bad is going to happen."

Truth: "God goes before me and surrounds me."

Thought: "I'm alone."

Truth: "God is with me and for me."

Your thoughts influence your emotions, so if you want to feel differently, you must think differently. This is not toxic positivity — this is spiritual discipline.

Today, we begin training your mind like a muscle — consistent, intentional, repetitive truth.

Bible Reading

Journal Prompt:

What thought do you need to take

captive today?

Every time an anxious thought rises, say out loud: "This thought submits to Christ."
Use the space below to document the response you notice in your thoughts and
mind.

Your mind can only hold one dominant thought at a time. That means every moment you're focused on truth is a moment anxiety loses its grip. Truth doesn't just silence fear — it overrides it.

Joshua 1:9 commands us: "Do not be afraid; do not be discouraged." But God doesn't stop there. He gives the reason: "For the Lord your God is with you wherever you go."

Fear says: "You're on your own."

Truth says: "God is with you."

Fear says: "This will end badly."

Truth says: "God makes all things work together for good."

Fear says: "You don't have what it takes."

Truth says: "God equips those He calls."

Anxiety thrives in silence — when you let fearful thoughts run free without interruption. But truth spoken out loud breaks the cycle.

Today's work: replacing fear with truth immediately.

Don't wait until the spiral starts.

Don't wait until you're overwhelmed.

Don't wait until anxiety has gripped your chest.

Interrupt fear as soon as it whispers.

Speak truth as soon as fear breathes.

Truth isn't a suggestion.

Truth is a weapon.

READ, REFLECT, & PRAY ON
JOSHUA 1:9 (KJV)

Journal Prompt:

What truth from Scripture do you need

to anchor yourself in today?

Today's Challenge

Write a "Truth Declaration" that begins with:
"I will not fear because God..."
Finish it with your own words

You cannot expect a peaceful life while living with an anxious thought pattern. Peace isn't something you stumble into — it's something you practice. And Philippians 4:8 tells you exactly how to practice it.

Think about what is true.

Think about what is noble.

Think about what is right, pure, lovely, admirable, excellent, praiseworthy. That's not just a poetic list — it's a filter.

A guide.

A mental strategy.

When an anxious thought appears, ask:

• Is this true?

• Is this helpful?

• Is this aligned with Scripture?

• Is this leading me to peace?

If the answer is no — reject it and replace it.

Practicing peaceful thinking doesn't mean bad things don't happen. It means you refuse to mentally live in disaster before anything even occurs.

Peace is not denial.

Peace is direction.

Your thoughts will go wherever you steer them. Today, choose to steer them toward peace intentionally.

Bible Reading

Journal Prompt:

Which of the Philippians 4:8 filters do you

struggle with the most?

Write one "peace phrase" you can repeat during anxious moments. Example: "I choose thoughts that bring peace, not panic."

Isaiah 26:3 says, "You will keep in perfect peace those whose minds are stayed on You."

Stayed. Focused. Rooted.

Perfect peace isn't random — it's trained.

Your mind naturally drifts toward fear, what-ifs, and anxieties. That's the result of past wounds, old habits, spiritual warfare, and lived experiences. But God teaches you how to train your mind toward peace.

Training looks like:
· Redirecting your thoughts every time they wander
· Speaking Scripture out loud
· Practicing gratitude in anxious moments
· Meditating on God's character instead of your fears
· Interrupting spirals with worship
· Choosing truth over imagination

Every time you redirect your mind, you are strengthening spiritual muscles that once felt weak.

Training takes repetition, consistency, and grace for yourself on the hard days.

But over time, your mind becomes less reactive and more rooted. Less chaotic and more anchored. Less anxious and more aligned with God's peace.

**READ, REFLECT, & PRAY ON
ISAIAH 26:3 (KJV)**

Journal Prompt:

Where does your mind drift when you're

not paying attention?

Spend five minutes today meditating on Isaiah 26:3.
Slowly.
Deliberately.
Invite God to train your mind.

Weekly Recap

This week shifted the focus from your emotions to your thoughts — and that's where real transformation begins. Anxiety may start in your body, but it lives in your mind. And this week, you began reclaiming that territory. You learned to identify fearful thoughts, take them captive, replace them with truth, and redirect your mind toward peace.

Take a moment to acknowledge the progress you've made.
Your thoughts may not be perfectly calm — but they're not running wild like they used to. You're becoming aware. You're interrupting spirals. You're practicing truth. That is spiritual maturity. That is growth. That is renewal.

Ask yourself:
· Which thought patterns were the hardest to break this week?
· Which truths felt the most powerful when spoken out loud?
· Where did you notice peace beginning to rise?

This journey isn't about never having anxious thoughts again — it's about responding to them differently. With authority. With Scripture. With clarity. With confidence.

Celebrate the shifts, even the small ones.
Your mind is learning a new way to think.
And that means your life is learning a new way to live.

Weekly Challenge

Every morning this week, start your day with a 2-minute "Thought Reset."
Here's how:

1. Identify one anxious thought you woke up with.

2. Ask, "Is this true?"

3. Replace it out loud with Scripture.

4. Redirect your focus toward gratitude.

This small routine rewires your mind to choose peace before anxiety has a chance to build momentum.

Then, each evening, ask yourself:
"What thought tried to take over today — and how did I respond?"

You're not aiming for perfection.
You're aiming for awareness and alignment.

By the end of this week, you'll notice how quickly your mind turns toward truth — and how much weaker anxiety feels because of it.

Weekly Prayer

Dear Lord,

Renew my mind with Your truth.

Teach me to recognize anxious thoughts quickly and replace them with Scripture.

Strengthen me to choose peace, even when fear rises.

Help me focus my mind on what is true, noble, and praiseworthy.

Anchor me in Your presence and steady my heart when my thoughts wander.

Thank You for transforming me from the inside out.

In Jesus' name,
Amen.

Week Four

There are fears that feel small — the ones you can shrug off, breathe through, or talk yourself out of. And then there are the fears that hit like a tidal wave, knocking the breath out of your lungs and leaving you wondering how you'll ever stand again. It's those moments Isaiah 41:10 speaks to: "Do not fear, for I am with you... I will strengthen you and help you."

Fear becomes overwhelming when you forget you're not facing it alone.

Some fears feel too big because you're looking at them through your own strength. You're asking, "How will I get through this?" when God is saying, "You won't — We will." Your strength isn't the source. Your wisdom isn't the source. Your ability to predict outcomes isn't the source.

God is.

When something feels too big for you, that's because it is.
But nothing is too big for the One who holds you.

Fear doesn't disappear because the situation changes. Fear loses power when your focus shifts from the problem to the God who promised to walk you through it.

Today, let God remind you that you don't have to be fearless — you just have to be held.

READ ISAIAH 41:10 (KJV)

Spend time praying right now that God reveals to you what fear feels "too big" for you right now?

Journal your thoughts below. Identify which of your worries are real and which are just created to distract you from your purpose and calling.

Speak Isaiah 41:10 aloud three times today as a declaration of God's presence and strength.

You can love God deeply and still walk through a valley that terrifies you. Loving Jesus doesn't exempt you from fear — it equips you for it. Psalm 23:4 says, "Even though I walk through the valley of the shadow of death, I will fear no evil, for You are with me." Notice: God doesn't say you'll avoid valleys. He says you won't walk them alone.

Maybe your valley was a diagnosis.

Maybe it was a loss you never saw coming.

Maybe it was betrayal, uncertainty, heartbreak, disappointment.

Maybe it was the moment the life you knew shattered.

There was a moment in my life when fear hit so hard, I felt like the floor dropped out from under me. The kind of fear that goes straight through your body. The kind that leaves you shaking. The kind that makes every breath a prayer you can barely get out.

And yet... God was there.

Not shouting.

Not condemning.

Just present.

Just steady.

Just enough.

Fear will try to break you, but God will always hold you.

He doesn't promise a life without shadows — He promises a Shepherd who walks with you through them. Your comfort isn't in the absence of danger; your comfort is in the presence of God.

Bible Reading

READ PSALM 23:4 (KJV)

Read the scripture then spend time in prayer asking
God to reveal to you what valley are you walking through
right now?

Answer this question below: Where have you mislabeled
worry as wisdom, responsibility, or preparation?

Today's Challenge

Invite God into the exact place fear tried to take you out.

There are days when trusting God feels like the easiest, most natural thing in the world — and then there are days when trust feels impossible. Days when the prayer you prayed didn't get answered the way you hoped. Days when your life didn't go in the direction you thought it would. Days when disappointment makes you question everything you thought you knew.

Proverbs 3:5 says, "Trust in the Lord with all your heart and lean not on your own understanding."

Not some of your heart.

Not half.

All.

But trusting God with all your heart feels hard when your understanding is screaming, "But this doesn't make sense!"

Here's the truth:

Trust doesn't require understanding.

Trust requires surrender.

You don't have to understand the situation to trust the One who leads you through it. Trust grows in uncertainty. Trust deepens in confusion. Trust strengthens when life feels unstable — because trust isn't rooted in circumstances. It's rooted in God's character.

When trust feels impossible, don't force yourself to feel strong. Bring God the part of your heart that's struggling. He can work with honesty. He can work with pain. He can work with doubt. He can work with tears.

He can't work with pretending.

READ PROVERBS 3:5 (KJV)

Which part of your heart is struggling to trust God right now? Take some time to pray over this scripture with a heart that seeks God's will and clarity. Journal your thoughts and answers below.

Today's Challenge

Pray, "God, I trust You with the part of my heart that doesn't understand," and name the specific fear or question you've been holding onto. Then take one small step of obedience this week that shows you truly believe He is faithful, even when you don't have all the answers.

Day 4 – The Fear Follows The Bad News

There's a unique kind of fear that hits when life blindsides you with bad news. It's the fear that settles deep in your chest. The fear that wakes you up at night. The fear that tries to rewrite your future before anything has actually happened. The fear that whispers, "This is it. Everything is about to fall apart."

Nahum 1:7 says, "The Lord is good, a refuge in times of trouble. He cares for those who trust in Him."

Trouble may show up, but so does God.

When my family received news that changed everything, fear came fast. It wasn't gentle. It wasn't subtle. It was overwhelming. But at the same time, there was a strange strength beneath it — not from me, but from God. A quiet assurance that even though life had shifted, God hadn't.

Fear follows bad news — but God follows you.

He goes into the diagnosis room.

He sits with you in the waiting.

He stands beside you when the doctor says something you never wanted to hear.

He surrounds you when your heart breaks.

He stays when fear rises.

Fear wants you to imagine the worst. God wants you to remember who He is: good, steady, unwavering, present.

READ NAHUM 1:7 (KJV)

What do you think today's reading means in the context of your life? What "bad news" moment still grips your heart with fear?
Journal your thoughts below after reading and spending time in prayer.

Today's Challenge

What "bad news" moment still grips your heart with fear?

There's a kind of peace that makes sense — the kind you feel when everything is going well, when life is calm, when the future looks bright. And then there's God's peace — the kind that makes absolutely no sense in the middle of the storm. The kind that shows up when circumstances don't change, but you do. The kind that guards your heart when fear says you should be falling apart.

Philippians 4:7 calls it the peace that surpasses understanding.
Peace that doesn't need answers.
Peace that doesn't need certainty.
Peace that isn't based on circumstances.
Peace that comes from God Himself.

This peace isn't fragile.
It's not temporary.
It's not emotional.
It's supernatural.

You can be shaking and still be held.
You can be crying and still be covered.
You can be uncertain and still be anchored.

Fear says, "You can't get through this."
Peace says, "Watch God carry you."

When faith and fear collide, let God meet you with peace that doesn't require your understanding — just your surrender.

READ PHILLIPIANS 4:7 (KJV)

Spend time reading this scripture and going to God in prayer. Journal your thoughts and revelations below. Be sure to answer the question: When was the last time you experienced peace that didn't match your situation?

Today's Challenge

Spend three minutes today in silence, asking God for peace that surpasses understanding. Journal below what peace will look like for you in those situations.

Weekly Recap

This week took you straight into the places where fear feels the strongest. You didn't avoid the hard moments. You didn't pretend your fears weren't real. You faced them — and you found God in the middle of every one of them.

Fear may not disappear overnight, but this week proved something powerful:
Fear does not get the final say.

God does.

As you reflect, ask yourself:
· Which fear did God speak into the loudest?
· What moment from this week changed how you see His presence?
· Where did faith rise even when fear tried to overwhelm you?

Maybe your valley isn't over.
Maybe the diagnosis is still there.
Maybe the situation hasn't changed.
But you have.
Your trust deepened.
Your awareness shifted.
Your peace grew stronger.

God meets you in the collision between faith and fear — not to shame you, but to strengthen you. He walks into the places that scare you and holds you while the storm rages.

Let this week remind you:
Fear may shout, but God speaks louder.
Fear may rise, but God remains.
Fear may attack, but God protects.

You are not walking through any of this alone.

Choose one fear that rose up this week — the one that felt the strongest or the most overwhelming — and confront it with Scripture daily. Write it down, along with one verse that directly contradicts it. Speak that verse out loud every morning and every evening. Let truth become louder than fear.

Then ask yourself each night:
"Where did I choose faith today, even in a small way?"

Faith isn't always a roaring declaration. Sometimes it's a whisper:
"God, I trust You anyway."
By the end of the week, you'll begin to notice that fear feels smaller — not because your situation changed, but because your confidence in God grew.

Dear Father,

Thank You for meeting me in the places where faith and fear collide.

Strengthen my heart when fear rises and remind me of Your presence when I feel overwhelmed.

Teach me to trust You in every valley, every uncertainty, and every moment of bad news.

Cover me with peace that surpasses understanding, and anchor me in Your love.

Help me lean on Your strength instead of my own. I surrender every fear into Your hands.

In Jesus' name,
Amen.

Week Five

Day 1: The Real Battle That You're Fighting

You can't defeat what you don't understand — and anxiety is more than a feeling. Ephesians 6:12 reminds us that "our struggle is not against flesh and blood" but against spiritual powers working behind the scenes. That means the battle you're fighting isn't just in your body or mind. The enemy aims straight for your thoughts because he knows your mind is the gateway to your peace, your purpose, and your confidence.

Anxiety whispers lies that sound like your own voice.

It exaggerates threats that aren't real.

It repeats fears until they feel like truth.

It wears you down until you forget the authority you carry.

Sis, the enemy attacks your mind because he fears what you'll become if you ever walk in full peace and clarity.

But here's the truth the enemy hopes you never discover:

You're not fighting for victory — you're fighting from victory. Jesus already defeated the enemy. Your role is to stand firm, resist the lies, and speak truth with authority.

Today, instead of seeing anxiety as a personal weakness, see it for what it is: spiritual warfare aimed at stopping you. And you don't fight spiritual battles with self-help. You fight with scripture, praise, prayer, and the power of God.

READ EPHESIANS 6:10-18 (KJV)

Spend time praying right now that God reveal to you and answer this. Where have you been fighting anxiety in your own strength instead of spiritually?

Today's Challenge

Write out Ephesians 6:10–18 below. Highlight every weapon God gives you.

The enemy doesn't need to destroy you.
He just needs to deceive you.

John 8:44 tells us Satan is "the father of lies." That means lying isn't just something he does — it's literally his nature. And anxiety is one of his favorite strategies to deliver those lies straight to your mind.

Lie: "You're not safe."

Lie: "Something bad is coming."

Lie: "You're not strong enough."

Lie: "God won't come through."

Lie: "You're alone in this."

These lies feel real because the enemy wraps them in emotion. He'll attach fear to a thought so it feels true even when it isn't.

But here's the truth:

Every anxious lie collapses under the weight of God's Word.
When Jesus was tempted in the wilderness, He didn't negotiate.

He didn't panic.

He didn't spiral.

He said three words: "It is written."

You can't outthink the enemy — but you can defeat him with truth.
When anxiety rises, you answer it with scripture, not fear.

READ JOHN 8:24 (KJV)

Read the scripture then spend time in prayer asking God to reveal to you which lie anxiety uses most often to attack you.

Today's Challenge

Write one verse that crushes that lie. Speak it out loud three times today.

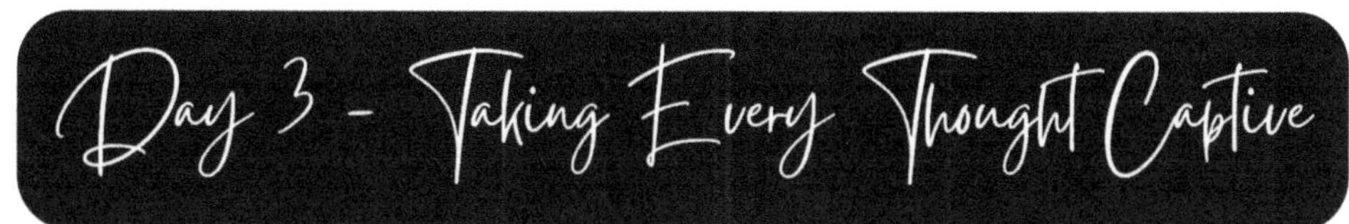

Scripture says the weapons we fight with are not of this world.
That means you're not fighting anxiety with personality, willpower, or coping mechanisms.
You're fighting with divine power.

2 Corinthians 10:4–5 says we "demolish arguments" and take "every thought captive."
Demolish means destroy completely, tear down, uproot. Not analyze. Not entertain. Not tolerate.

Sis, you don't manage anxious thoughts — you take them captive.
Taking a thought captive means:

· You stop it the moment it appears

· You examine it under the truth of God's Word

· You decide whether it aligns with God's voice

· If not, you cast it out immediately

· You replace it with truth

This is spiritual discipline.
This is mental warfare.
This is how you stop anxiety from building strongholds.

Thought: "I can't handle this."
Truth: "God is my strength."

Thought: "What if everything goes wrong?"
Truth: "God works all things together for good."

Thought: "I'm alone."
Truth: "God will never leave me nor forsake me."

Bible Reading

What thought needs to be taken captive right now? Take some time to pray over this scripture with a heart that seeks God's will and clarity. Journal your thoughts and answers below.

Every time an anxious thought rises today, say: "Thought, you do not belong to me." Document below the thought, the lie, and the truth.

You don't fight anxiety with logic.
You fight anxiety with the Word of God.

Hebrews 4:12 says the Word is "alive and active… sharper than any double-edged sword." That means scripture isn't just comforting — it's powerful. It cuts through lies. It exposes fear. It breaks strongholds. It silences the enemy.

When Jesus faced Satan's attack, He didn't quote motivational sayings.
He quoted scripture.
Because scripture isn't just information — it's a weapon.

That's why anxiety rises when you're spiritually dry.
That's why fear attacks when you stop reading the Word.
That's why the enemy distracts you from Scripture — because he knows it destroys his influence over your mind.

Today, your assignment is practical and spiritual:
We're building a Scripture Combat List — verses you speak when anxiety hits.

For example:

• When fear rises → Isaiah 41:10

• When worry spirals → Philippians 4:6–7

• When uncertainty overwhelms → Proverbs 3:5–6

• When lies scream → John 8:44

• When peace feels impossible → Isaiah 26:3

• When you feel alone → Deuteronomy 31:8

Bible Reading

READ HEBREWS 4:12 (KJV)

What do you think today's reading means in the context of your life? Which scripture speaks the loudest to your fear right now? Journal your thoughts below after reading and spending time in prayer.

Write your Scripture Combat List and keep it somewhere visible.

Day 5 – You Fight From Victory, Not For It

Anxiety feels powerful — but it's not more powerful than the Spirit of God inside you.
1 John 4:4 says, "Greater is He that is in you than he that is in the world."

The enemy wants you to believe you're losing.
God wants you to know you've already won.

You don't fight anxiety alone.
You don't fight anxiety unarmed.
You don't fight anxiety weak or helpless — you fight with the power of the One who defeated the enemy forever.

Anxiety grows when you think the battle depends on you.
Peace grows when you remember the battle belongs to God.

This truth changes everything:
You fight from victory, not for it.

Jesus already conquered fear.
Jesus already defeated the enemy.

Jesus already broke the power of lies.
Jesus already secured your peace.

Your job is not to win — your job is to stand.

Stand firm.
Stand in truth.
Stand in faith.
Stand in identity.
Stand in authority.
Stand knowing the outcome is already settled.

Spend time reading this scripture and going to
God in prayer. Identify where you have been acting
like victory depends on you. Journal your thoughts
and revelations below.

Today's Challenge

Speak this declaration today:
"I fight from victory because Jesus has already won."

Weekly Recap

This week opened your eyes to the spiritual reality behind anxiety. You've learned that anxiety isn't just a feeling you need to manage — it's a battle you're equipped to win. You saw how the enemy uses lies, fear, and mental attacks to weaken your peace. But more importantly, you discovered the authority God has given you to fight back.

Your mind is valuable. Your peace is powerful. Your calling is dangerous to the enemy — and that's why he fights so hard. But this week, you didn't shrink back. You recognized the lies. You confronted the thoughts. You spoke scripture. You fought spiritually instead of emotionally.

Pause and reflect:
- What lie did you finally expose?
- Which scripture became a weapon for you?
- Where did you sense God strengthening you?
- What moment did you feel spiritual clarity instead of confusion?

You are learning to fight differently — and that's changing everything.
The enemy may attack, but he cannot win.
You may feel fear, but you will not fall.
Your mind may be a battleground, but it is also a place of victory.

This week, God didn't just calm your anxiety — He equipped you for battle.

Weekly Challenge

This week, choose ONE area where anxiety has controlled your thoughts and apply a daily spiritual strategy to it. Here's your simple plan:

1. Identify the lie.

2. Find a verse that crushes it.

3. Speak that verse out loud every morning and evening.

4. Reject the lie immediately each time it appears.

5. Replace it with truth — out loud.

This is not a mental exercise — this is spiritual warfare. Consistency is the weapon. Scripture is the sword. Your voice is the breakthrough. By the end of this week, you'll notice your reactions shifting. The fear will feel weaker. The lie will feel exposed. And truth will begin to take deeper root.

Weekly Prayer

Dear Father,

Thank You for giving me authority over every lie, fear, and attack of the enemy.

Strengthen me to stand firm when anxiety rises.

Open my eyes to the spiritual battle around me and remind me that You have already won.

Fill my mind with truth and guard my heart with peace.
Teach me to fight with Scripture, with prayer, and with bold confidence in Your power.

I renounce every lie and cling to Your Word.

In Jesus' name,
Amen.

Week Six

Let's be honest — waiting is one of the hardest parts of the Christian walk. You pray, you believe, you try to stay strong, but then days turn into months, months turn into years, and you start wondering, "Did God forget me?" When life moves slowly, anxiety moves quickly. It fills the gaps with fear, doubt, and "what ifs."

Psalm 27:14 tells us: "Wait for the Lord; be strong and take heart and wait for the Lord."

Waiting requires strength because waiting requires trust.

But God is not slow — He is strategic. He sees everything you can't. He's preparing people, aligning circumstances, protecting you from things you don't know about yet. Just because you don't see movement doesn't mean God isn't moving.

The enemy loves to attack you during waiting seasons because he knows it's where your faith is stretched and shaped. He'll whisper:

"God must not care."
"God must not be listening."
"God must not be coming."

Sis, don't mistake silence for absence.

God is not late.
He's not stalling.
He's not uncertain.
He's preparing.

When God feels slow, remember this:

Waiting is not wasted.
Waiting is working.
Waiting is strengthening.

READ PSALM 27:14 (KJV)

Spend time praying right now that God reveal to you where the enemy is attacking your mind. Where have you felt like God is moving too slowly? Journal your thoughts below.

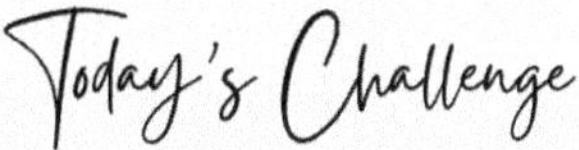

Speak this aloud: "God is never late — He is preparing something I can't see yet."

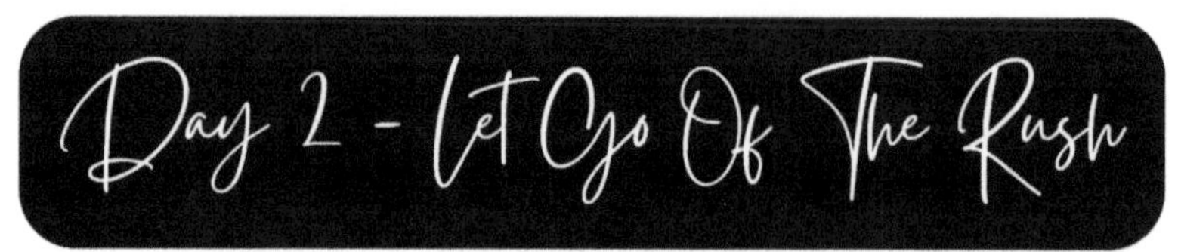

"Hurry" is one of the enemy's loudest strategies. Hurry keeps you stressed. Hurry keeps you distracted. Hurry convinces you that everything has to be figured out right now or something terrible will happen. And hurry is where anxiety thrives.

Psalm 46:10 says, "Be still, and know that I am God."

Stillness is not inactivity — it's intentional calm. It's choosing not to panic. It's choosing to slow your breathing, slow your thoughts, slow your reactions, and center yourself in God's presence.

When you're rushing, you're reacting.
When you're still, you're listening.

Stillness creates space for God to speak.
Hurry creates noise that drowns His voice out.

God is never in a rush. He doesn't panic when you feel behind. He doesn't stress when a deadline feels impossible. He doesn't worry about timing — and neither should you.

Today, practice slowing down. Slow your steps. Slow your tone. Slow your decisions. Slow your pace. The world will keep rushing, but you don't have to follow it.

Bible Reading

Read the scripture then spend time in prayer asking
God to reveal to you where is hurry creating anxiety in
your life?

Today's Challenge

Take five minutes today to sit in silence with God. No talking. No praying. Just breathing and being.

One of the most comforting truths about God's timing is this: it's protective. God sees everything — the conversations you didn't hear, the obstacles ahead, the opportunities that aren't ready, the people who need time to grow, and the dangers He's shielding you from. When God delays something, it's never punishment. It's protection.

Isaiah 55:8–9 reminds us that His ways are higher than ours. That means His timing isn't based on your feelings, your expectations, or your deadlines — it's based on His perfect wisdom.

Some of the biggest heartbreaks in life come from things you tried to force before their time. And some of your greatest blessings came right when you thought God was too late.

If only you could see what God has kept you from...

the wrong relationships,

the unstable opportunities,

the unprepared environments,

the spiritual battles you weren't ready to face.

.

If God hasn't opened the door yet, it's because what's behind it isn't ready — or because you aren't ready yet.

He's not denying you.

He's protecting you.

READ ISAIAH 55:8-9 (KJV)

What area of your life might God be protecting through delayed timing? Take some time to pray over this scripture with a heart that seeks God's will and clarity. Journal your thoughts and answers below.

Write a prayer thanking God for the doors He has NOT opened yet.

There is a deep kind of peace that comes when you can look at a situation that hasn't changed and still say, "God is good. God is faithful. God is working." That's maturity. That's trust. That's surrender.

Lamentations 3:25–26 says, "The Lord is good to those who wait for him... It is good to wait quietly for the salvation of the Lord."

Good.
Not frustrating
Not painful.
Not pointless.
Good.

Waiting becomes good when you trust the One you're waiting on.

The "not yet" is often where God does His greatest work — in your heart, your character, your faith, your strength. If God gave you the blessing instantly, you'd miss the transformation that prepares you to carry it.

Trusting God in the "not yet" looks like:

· releasing your timeline

· refusing to panic

· surrendering the urge to control

· choosing gratitude over grumbling

· worshipping while you wait

· believing God's goodness before you see His answer

Your blessing is not just the thing you're waiting for — your blessing is who you're becoming in the process.

Bible Reading

READ LAMENTATIONS 3:25-26
(KJV)

Where in your life are you living in a "not yet"
Journal your thoughts below after reading and
spending time in prayer.

Speak this declaration: "God is working in my waiting, even when I can't see it."

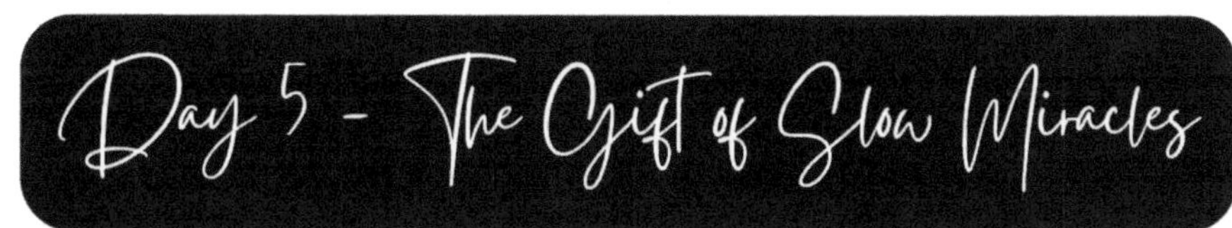

God's peace doesn't just comfort you—*it guards you.*

His peace stands watch over your heart like a divine security detail assigned to protect your mind from intruding thoughts.

That's not poetic exaggeration—that's **Scripture**.

Peace is not passive.

Peace has an agenda: *to keep you safe.*

But peace can only guard **what you actually give over to God.**

- If you're still clutching the problem, *peace can't cover it.*
  - If you're still rehearsing the fear, *peace can't replace it.*
    - If you're still carrying what wasn't meant for you, *peace can't lighten the load.*

Think of peace like standing under an umbrella in a storm. *The storm doesn't disappear because you stepped under it—but you're protected.* You stop being drenched by the fear that used to soak you.

The more you trust God, the more ground peace covers.

Today, imagine peace covering your mind like a blanket—*warm, protective, steadying.*

Imagine peace guarding your thoughts like a shield.

Imagine peace holding back the flood of anxiety that once overwhelmed you.

Listen to me friend - **you are not called to be anxious.**

You are called to be guarded by a peace that only comes from your creator.

READ ECCLESIASTES 3:11 (KJV)

Spend time reading this scripture and going to God in prayer. Identify what slow miracle has God been forming in your life? Journal your thoughts and revelations below.

Today's Challenge

Write down one area where you see slow, steady progress — and thank God for it.

Weekly Recap

This week invited you to step out of the pressure of your own timing and into the peace of God's. You learned that hurry fuels anxiety, while stillness fuels clarity. You discovered that God isn't slow — He's protective. He isn't absent — He's preparing. He isn't withholding — He's working on something deeper, something better, something you may not fully understand yet.

As you look back over the week, reflect on these questions:
· What area did God ask you to release your timeline?
· Where did you feel Him calming the rush inside you?
· What slow miracle do you sense unfolding right now?
· How did your perspective of waiting begin to shift?

Waiting doesn't mean God is inactive.
Waiting means God is intentional.

He sees the big picture while you see the next step. He knows what needs to align, who needs to grow, what needs to heal, and when the timing will be perfect. God is not late — He is strategic, steady, and wise.

Let this week remind you that the same God who timed your breath, your birth, your breakthroughs, and your healing — will time this next chapter perfectly too.

Weekly Challenge

Choose one area of your life where you've been rushing God's timing — a prayer request, a relationship, a financial need, a dream, a healing, or a breakthrough. Write it down on a piece of paper and place it somewhere visible.

Every day this week, pray this simple prayer over it:
"Lord, I release the timeline. I trust Your pace. I trust Your process. I trust Your plan."

Each time anxiety rises and tells you you're falling behind, respond with:
"God is not late. God is preparing me. God is preparing the promise."

This daily practice will retrain your heart to trust God's timing over your own.

Weekly Prayer

Dear Father,

Teach me to trust Your timing.

Help me release the rush, the pressure, and the fear of falling behind.

Remind me that You are never early, never late, and always working for my good.

Calm my anxious heart and anchor me in Your pace.

Give me eyes to see slow miracles and strength to wait with patience and faith.

I surrender my timeline and rest in Your perfect timing.

In Jesus' name,
Amen.

Week Seven

Your spirit may trust God, but sometimes your body is still responding to trauma, stress, or chronic fear. Your shoulders tense. Your stomach drops. Your heart races. Your breath shortens. Your body speaks—often before your mind even recognizes what's happening.

3 John 1:2 says, "I pray that you may prosper in all things and be in health, just as your soul prospers."

This reveals something powerful: your physical health matters to God. He designed your body to live in sync with His peace.

But if you've lived in survival mode for years, your body may still be reacting to old wounds. Anxiety patterns get stored in your nervous system. They turn into physical habits: hypervigilance, shallow breathing, tight muscles, fatigue.

This does not mean you're weak.
 It means you're human.

God wants to heal the anxiety stored in your body — not just the anxiety you think about. That means:

• learning to slow your breathing
• letting your shoulders relax
• unclenching your jaw
• taking breaks
• nourishing your body
• recognizing physical triggers
• creating rhythms of rest, not rush

Your body needs peace just as much as your spirit does.

READ 3 JOHN 1:2 (KJV)

Spend time praying right now that God reveal
to you where anxiety shows up in your body.
Journal your thoughts below.

Today's Challenge

Today, pause three times to scan your body and release tension with slow, deep breaths.

Day 2 – Your Mind Needs Gentle Care

Your mind is powerful, but it is also sensitive. If your thoughts have lived in chaos for years, they need gentleness — not judgment. They need compassion — not criticism. Romans 8:6 says, "The mind governed by the Spirit is life and peace." That means peace is possible, but it must be cultivated.

Mental healing doesn't happen by force.
It happens by direction.

Your mind heals when you:

· interrupt spirals gently
· guide your thoughts toward truth
· challenge anxious predictions
· use gratitude to re-center your focus
· practice mental rest
· set boundaries
· stop letting your mind relive old pain

Sis, your mind needs recovery time. You can't pour Scripture over exhaustion and expect instant peace. You must slow down, breathe, and speak truth with kindness to yourself.

God is patient with your healing — you should be too.

This is what mental renewal looks like:

· "I feel fear, but fear is not the truth."
· "I'm overwhelmed, but I'm not alone."
· "My thoughts are racing, but I can redirect them."
· "I don't have to figure everything out right now."

Your mind becomes peaceful through repetition, not perfection.

Bible Reading

READ ROMANS 8:6 (KJV)

Read the scripture then spend time in prayer asking God to tell you what anxious thought shows up most often when you're mentally tired?

Once you've identified the thought from the previous page, replace that thought with a gentle truth every time it appears today.

Anxiety weakens your spirit just as much as it affects your body and mind. You start feeling spiritually foggy, disconnected, numb, or distant. You might still love God deeply — but feel tired inside. Psalm 23:3 says, "He restores my soul."

Restoration isn't a one-time event.
It's a daily process.

Your spirit needs nourishment just like your body does. You wouldn't eat once a week and expect to feel strong physically — you shouldn't nourish your spirit once a week either.

Spiritual nourishment looks like:

· reading Scripture slowly (not rushing it)
· worshipping even when emotions fluctuate
· talking to God honestly
· praying short prayers throughout the day
· resting instead of striving
· journaling what God is teaching you
· receiving comfort instead of trying to push through

You can't force spiritual growth, but you can create space for it. When your spirit is nourished, you feel:

· grounded
· more attentive to God's voice
· less reactive
· more hopeful
· more peaceful
· more resilient
· less overwhelmed by fear

Your spirit doesn't need pressure — it needs presence.
God restores what anxiety has drained.

READ PSALMS 23:3 (KJV)

Which spiritual practice brings you the most peace right now? Take some time to pray over this scripture with a heart that seeks God's will and clarity. Journal your thoughts and answers below.

Today's Challenge

Spend 10 quiet minutes with God today — no agenda, no hurry. no distractions, just you and God.

Day 4 – Aligning Body, Mind, And Spirit

Mark 12:30 says to love God with all your heart, soul, mind, and strength — because God created you as an integrated being. Everything affects everything. Your body affects your thoughts. Your thoughts affect your spirit. Your spirit affects your emotions. You cannot heal one and ignore the others.

When your body is exhausted, your thoughts spiral faster.
When your thoughts are anxious, your body becomes tense.
When your spirit is weary, your mind becomes vulnerable.
When your mind is overwhelmed, your body reacts physically.

Healing requires alignment.
Body care is spiritual.
Mental rest is spiritual.
Emotional honesty is spiritual.
Physical boundaries are spiritual.

Praying while your nervous system is overloaded is like trying to worship in the middle of a hurricane — the desire is real, but the overwhelm is louder.

This is why God addresses the whole person.

Today, ask yourself:

· What does my body need?
· What does my mind need?
· What does my spirit need?

They don't need the same thing every day.
Some days your body needs rest.
Some days your mind needs truth.
Some days your spirit needs worship.
Some days you need all three.

Healing happens when you honor each part with kindness.

READ MARK 12:30 (KJV)

Which part of you — body, mind, or spirit — needs
the most attention right now? Journal your thoughts
below after reading and spending time in prayer.

Choose one caring action today (stretching, drinking water, journaling, worship, a walk, deep breathing).

Isaiah 58:11 promises, "The Lord will guide you continually, giving you water when you are dry and restoring your strength." This is a picture of whole-person peace — not just emotional relief, but restoration in every part of your being.

Today we're creating a Peace Inventory — a simple, powerful tool to help you see where anxiety is creeping in and where God is already working.

Rate each area from 1–5 (1 = low, 5 = strong):

BODY:
· Sleep
· Tension levels
· Healthy movement
· Nutrition
· Restfulness

MIND:
· Thought patterns
· Ability to redirect spirals
· Overwhelm level
· Focus
· Calmness

SPIRIT:
· Awareness of God's presence
· Time in Scripture
· Worship
· Prayer
· Hopefulness

Where you score lowest is where you need the most tenderness, not shame. Healing is not about judgment — it's about clarity.

You'll start to recognize patterns:
"I'm anxious because I'm exhausted."
"I'm spiraling because my thoughts are unfocused."
"I feel overwhelmed because my spirit feels dry."

This inventory gives you a picture of your internal health — and helps you partner with God in areas where healing is rising.

READ ISAIAH 58:11 (KJV)

Spend time reading this scripture and going to God in prayer. Which category (body, mind, or spirit) scored the lowest? Journal your thoughts and revelations below.

Choose one small action today to raise your lowest score by even one point.

Weekly Recap

This week invited you to pay attention to parts of yourself you may have ignored, pushed down, or rushed through. Anxiety often blinds you to what your body feels, what your mind needs, and what your spirit longs for. But God sees all of it — and He cares deeply about every part.

Take a moment to reflect on what you learned:

· Where did you feel tension begin to release?

· Where did your thoughts become clearer?

· Where did your spirit feel nourished?

· What surprised you?

· What felt uncomfortable but necessary?

Your healing is not linear, but it is happening. You're learning to listen to your body without fear, guide your mind gently, and nourish your spirit intentionally. You're learning that God's peace isn't shallow — it's holistic. It reaches into physical exhaustion, emotional overwhelm, mental spirals, and spiritual dryness.

Ask God to show you where He's already restoring you.
Ask Him to highlight the next step.
Ask Him to strengthen what feels weak.

You're becoming more whole.
More grounded.
More aware.
More peaceful.

This week wasn't just about healing anxiety — it was about healing you.

Weekly Challenge

Using your Peace Inventory, choose ONE area — body, mind, or spirit — to intentionally improve this week. Don't choose all three. Choose one. Healing happens when focus meets consistency.

Here are examples:

• If your body scored lowest: prioritize rest, deep breathing, gentle stretching, hydration, or movement.
• If your mind scored lowest: practice thought redirection, gratitude, journaling, or mental breaks.
• If your spirit scored lowest: spend daily time in Scripture, worship, or quiet prayer.
Your assignment is simple:

Do one caring action for that area every day this week.
Small steps create deep healing.
Consistency creates peace.

By the end of the week, you'll notice the difference — not because life got easier, but because you tended to the parts of yourself that needed attention.

Weekly Prayer

Dear Father,

Thank You for caring about my whole being — body, mind, and spirit.

Show me where I need healing and guide me with gentleness.

Restore my strength where I am weary.

Calm my thoughts where I am overwhelmed.

Refresh my spirit where I feel dry.

Teach me to honor every part of myself with compassion and wisdom.

Fill me with Your peace, wholeness, and rest.

In Jesus' name,
Amen.

Week Eight

Anxiety's first strategy is simple: pull you away from people.
It whispers:

"No one gets you."
"You're too much."
"They have their own problems."
"Just deal with it alone."
"They'll think you're a burden."

And before you realize it, you've started shrinking your world. You stop answering messages. You avoid conversations. You stay home instead of showing up. You tell everyone, "I'm good," even when everything inside you screams otherwise.

This is not an accident — it's an attack.

Ecclesiastes 4:9–10 reminds us, "Two are better than one… If either of them falls, one can help the other up."

The enemy knows if he can isolate you, he can overwhelm you.
But if you stay connected, he loses his advantage.

Anxiety feels heavier when you carry it alone.
Thoughts feel louder when no one knows what's happening.
Fear feels bigger when there's no one reminding you of truth.

You were never meant to fight your battles in silence.

Community isn't a luxury for Christians — it's a necessity.
It's spiritual protection.
It's emotional anchoring.
It's God's answer to the enemy's strategy.

READ ECCLESIASTES 4:9-10 (KJV)

Spend time praying right now that God reveal to you where the enemy is attacking your mind. Where has anxiety been pulling you into isolation? Journal your thoughts below.

Today's Challenge

Text one person today and admit you've had a hard week. Let someone in.

Day 2 – You Weren't Made To Heal Alone

Galatians 6:2 says, "Carry each other's burdens, and in this way you will fulfill the law of Christ."

Sis, if you were meant to carry everything alone, this verse wouldn't exist.

Healing happens through connection.
Strength grows through support.
Peace flows through community.

But anxiety often convinces you that needing help is weakness.
That opening up means you're failing.
That vulnerability is risky.
That letting people see the real you will push them away.

None of that is true.

God made community the place where healing multiplies. When you share your fears with someone who loves you, anxiety loses its shame. When someone prays over you, anxiety loses its volume. When someone sits with you in silence, anxiety loses its power.

Your healing is not just vertical (between you and God).
It's also horizontal (between you and others).

Some breakthroughs won't come through private prayer — they come when someone else prays with you. Some lies won't break in your head — they break when spoken out loud. Some battles aren't meant to be fought alone — they require someone holding your arms up when you're tired.

Isolation feels safer, but it's not healing.
Connection feels scary, but it restores you.

READ GALATIANS 6:2 (KJV)

Read the scripture then spend time in prayer asking God to reveal to who in your life helps you feel safe, seen, or supported? Write down ways how you can grow to be more connected with your community.

Share one specific fear or struggle with someone you trust this week.

James 5:16 says, "Confess your sins to one another and pray for one another, so that you may be healed."

Healing and honesty are connected.
Not perfection — honesty.

You don't have to unload your entire story on everyone, but you do need at least one or two people who know the real you: the strong parts, the struggling parts, the fearful parts, the hopeful parts.

Being known is healing because:

· it breaks shame
· it dismantles lies
· it interrupts isolation
· it replaces fear with truth
· it brings comfort
· it opens the door for prayer
· it reminds you you're not alone

For so long, anxiety taught you to hide. But healing requires light — and people bring that light into places you've kept in the dark.

Here's the truth:
You cannot heal in isolation from a wound created in loneliness.

There is a difference between privacy and hiding.

Privacy is healthy.
Hiding is harmful.

Hiding says, "If they see me, they'll leave."
Healing says, "If they see me, they can help."

Today, God is inviting you to step into deeper connection so He can heal what fear tried to isolate.

READ JAMES 5:16 (KJV)

What part of your story have you kept hidden
because of fear? Take some time to pray over this
scripture with a heart that seeks God's will and clarity.
Journal your thoughts and answers below.

Today's Challenge

Tell one trusted person something you've never said out loud.

Not everyone in your life is meant to walk closely with you — and that's okay. Healing requires safe people, not perfect people.

Proverbs 27:17 says, "As iron sharpens iron, so one person sharpens another." Some people sharpen you.

Some dull you.
Some drain you.
Some strengthen you.
Some confuse you.
Some calm you.

You need the ones who sharpen you.

A safe person is someone who:
· listens without judging
· encourages without pressuring
· tells you the truth without shaming
· prays with you and for you
· loves you without needing you to be perfect
· doesn't disappear when things get heavy
· speaks peace when anxiety speaks fear
· helps you see God when you feel blind to Him

Safe people are a gift from God — and sometimes they show up in unexpected places. You don't need a crowd to heal.

You need a circle.

Your "people" don't have to be many — they just have to be real.
Choose connection over perfection.
Choose community over isolation.
Choose vulnerability over hiding.

READ PROVERBS 27:17 (KJV)

Who in your life feels like "safe people" right now?
Journal your thoughts below after reading and
spending time in prayer.

Today's Challenge

Reach out and thank one safe person for walking with you.

God doesn't just suggest community — He commands it. Hebrews 10:24–25 says, "Let us consider how we may spur one another on… not giving up meeting together… but encouraging one another."

Why?

Because encouragement is oxygen to an anxious heart.
Because truth spoken by someone else hits different.
Because your faith gets stronger when it's connected to someone else's faith.
Because healing happens when love is shared, prayed, spoken, and lived out.

You don't have to be in a perfect season to be in community.
You don't have to be fully healed to show up.
You don't have to have your life together to belong.

Community is not for the polished — it's for the honest.

There was a moment when I walked into a room hurting so deeply I couldn't speak it. But the presence of other believers — their worship, their warmth, their prayers — calmed something in me I didn't even know how to articulate. Sometimes healing is less about words and more about presence.

God uses community to:

· lift you when you're down
· pray you through the valleys
· remind you of your worth
· challenge lies with truth
· call out the God in you
· strengthen your faith
· steady your heart

You are not meant to do this alone.
Let people help hold you together.

READ HEBREWS 10:24–25
(KJV)

Spend time reading this scripture and going to God in prayer. Where do you feel God calling you to lean into community instead of isolation? Journal your thoughts and revelations below.

Commit to attending or reaching out to a community gathering, group, or circle at least once this week.

Weekly Recap

This week revealed something crucial: anxiety isolates, but God heals through connection. You weren't designed to walk your battles alone, and you don't have to. God places the right people in your life at the right time to strengthen you, support you, speak truth to you, and walk with you through the valleys that feel too heavy to face by yourself.

Take time to reflect:

· Where did you feel anxiety pushing you toward isolation?
· How did God use someone to bring comfort, truth, or peace?
· What happened when you opened up instead of hiding?
· Who are the people you can trust with your heart?
· What does God want to show you about community?

You might be surprised by how much healing you experienced simply by telling someone the truth, receiving prayer, or allowing yourself to be seen. You may also realize that some of the fear you carried began to lose its hold the moment you shared it with another person.

Healing is a community assignment.
Growth is a community process.
Strength is a community outcome.
You are not alone — and you never were.

Let this week remind you that God uses people to heal people.

Weekly Challenge

Choose one way to intentionally practice connection this week. Here are options:

• Attend a small group or Bible study
• Reach out to a friend
• Share honestly with someone you trust
• Pray with another person
• Join a community space like Sisterhood or Mission Circles
• Invite someone to coffee and have a real conversation

Your goal is simple: do not hide.

Let at least one person into the real parts of your heart, even if it feels uncomfortable at first. Healing accelerates when you stop doing life alone.

Every time you choose connection, you are breaking one of anxiety's strongest weapons.

Weekly Prayer

Dear Father,

Thank You for surrounding me with people who reflect Your love.

Teach me to open my heart, share my burdens, and receive support without shame.

Break every pattern of isolation in my life and lead me into the relationships that bring healing, strength, and truth.

Help me recognize the community You've placed around me and give me courage to connect.

Heal the parts of me that hide and strengthen the parts that seek connection.

In Jesus' name,
Amen.

Week Nine

Day 1: Peace Is A Practice, Not a Personality

Some people look naturally calm, but peace is not a personality trait — it's a practice. Philippians 4:9 says, "Whatever you have learned or received or heard from me… put it into practice. And the God of peace will be with you."

Peace comes when you practice what God has taught you.

You do not drift into peace.
 You decide to stay there.
Every day, you are choosing between two patterns:

• the old pattern of fear
• the new pattern of trust

Your body may remember anxiety. Your mind may remember chaos. But your spirit remembers truth — and truth always has authority. Living unanxious means you intentionally put truth in the driver's seat.

This looks like:
• redirecting spirals immediately
• slowing down your reactions
• breathing before responding
• choosing gratitude over worry
• speaking Scripture out loud
• refusing to entertain worst-case scenarios
• protecting your environment
• saying "no" when your peace is at risk

Peace isn't something you magically wake up with; it's something you build through habits, decisions, boundaries, and alignment with God's Word.

The more you practice peace, the more natural it becomes — and the more unnatural anxiety becomes.

READ PHILIPPIANS 4:9 (KJV)

Spend time praying right now that God reveal to you where the enemy is attacking your mind. What peace practices have helped you the most so far? Journal your thoughts below.

Today's Challenge

Commit to practicing at least TWO peace habits today.

Proverbs 4:23 says, "Above all else, guard your heart, for everything you do flows from it."

Protecting your peace is not optional — it is spiritual responsibility. When your peace is unprotected, everything leaks: your energy, your clarity, your joy, your relationships, your purpose.

Peace requires boundaries.
Peace requires wisdom.
Peace requires discernment.

You can't maintain an unanxious life if you stay in anxious environments. You can't live in peace while surrounding yourself with people who drain you. You can't walk confidently while constantly exposing yourself to things that trigger fear, insecurity, or overwhelm.

Sometimes protecting your peace means:

· saying no without guilt
· stepping away from drama
· limiting access to draining people
· reducing noise (online and offline)
· choosing rest instead of rushing
· not responding immediately
· honoring your emotional capacity
· creating rhythms that support your nervous system

Peace is expensive — but anxiety costs more.

You owe it to yourself, your calling, and your relationship with God to protect what He's given you. God can hand you peace, but you must guard it.

READ PROVERBS 4:23 (KJV)

Read the scripture then spend time in prayer asking God to give you peace. Answer this question below: what environment or relationship has been stealing your peace?

Set one boundary today that supports your mental, emotional, or spiritual peace.

Day 3 – Spirit-Led Living is Anxiety's Opposite

Romans 8:14 says, "For those who are led by the Spirit of God are the children of God."

Anxiety pushes.
The Holy Spirit leads.

Anxiety rushes.
The Holy Spirit guides.

Anxiety pressures.
The Holy Spirit whispers.

Living unanxious means becoming more responsive to God's voice than your fear. When the Spirit leads, there is calm wisdom, quiet confidence, and steady clarity. When anxiety leads, there is urgency, panic, and confusion.

Spirit-led living looks like:
· pausing instead of reacting
· asking God before deciding
· moving only when you have peace
· trusting God with uncertainty
· obeying small nudges
· stepping back when God says wait
· staying grounded in His Word
· letting God's voice be louder than your emotions

Anxiety thrives where the Holy Spirit is ignored.
Peace thrives where the Holy Spirit is obeyed.

You don't have to guess your way through life. The Spirit is your guide, your comforter, your counselor, and your internal anchor. When you follow Him, anxiety loses its influence.

READ ROMANS 8:14 (KJV)

Where do you feel the Holy Spirit leading you right now? Take some time to pray over this scripture with a heart that seeks God's will and clarity. Journal your thoughts and answers below.

Pause today before every major decision and ask, "Holy Spirit, what do You want me to do?"

Day 4 – Your New Default: Peace, Not Panic

John 14:27 says, "Peace I leave with you; my peace I give you… Do not let your hearts be troubled and do not be afraid."

Jesus didn't suggest peace — He gave it.

Peace is your inheritance.

Peace is your normal.

Peace is your default setting.

But for many years, anxiety became your default because it was familiar. It was predictable. It was your survival system. Even when it hurt you, it felt normal.

This week is about shifting your identity:
You are not "an anxious person."
You are a peaceful person learning new patterns.

Living unanxious means panic is no longer your baseline. It means when trouble comes, your spirit responds before your fear does. It means your automatic response becomes:
• "God is here."
• "God is working."
• "God is covering me."
• "God goes before me."
• "God is not surprised."

Peace becomes your instinct, not panic.

This is the transformation God has been building in you over the last nine weeks — not just managing anxiety, but becoming a woman who walks in God's peace consistently.

READ JOHN 14:27 (KJV)

What do you think today's reading means in the context of your life? What would your life look like if peace were your default response?
Journal your thoughts below after reading and spending time in prayer.

Today's Challenge

Whenever panic rises today, immediately pause and speak John 14:27 out loud.

Isaiah 26:3 promises, "You will keep in perfect peace those whose minds are steadfast, because they trust in You."

Perfect peace is not perfection — it is consistency.

It is choosing trust again and again until trust becomes who you are.

Your new normal is not a life without challenges, but a life where challenges no longer shake you. It's waking up with clarity. It's responding with wisdom. It's refusing to let fear lead. It's noticing anxious thoughts but not obeying them.

Living unanxious means:

You know your triggers

You have tools before you need them

You protect your peace intentionally

You lean into God instead of isolating

You rest instead of rushing

You choose connection over hiding

You trust God more than you trust your imagination.

This is not the end of your healing — it's the beginning of your new lifestyle. A lifestyle where you don't survive anxiety, you overcome it. Where you don't manage your fear, you silence it. Where you don't crumble under pressure, you stand firm in God's strength.

This is who you are now.

This is your new normal.

READ ISAIAH 26:3 (KJV)

Spend time reading this scripture and going to God in prayer. What part of your new normal feels the most life-giving? Journal your thoughts and revelations below.

Today's Challenge

Write a declaration that begins with: "I am a woman of peace, and…"
Repeat it all week.

Weekly Recap

This week marks a shift in identity. You are no longer a woman shaped by anxiety — you are a woman strengthened by God's peace. You have learned not only how to calm your fear but how to cultivate a life where peace is protected, practiced, and prioritized.

Take time to reflect on what has changed in you:
• How has your thinking shifted?
• Where do you feel more grounded?
• What old patterns have lost their power?
• What new habits have anchored your peace?
• How has God shaped your responses, your pace, and your perspective?

Look back at who you were at the beginning of this study.
Look at who you are now.
There is a noticeable difference — in your strength, your clarity, your confidence, and the way you experience God.

This is not temporary.
This is transformation.

This study was not about eliminating every anxious thought, but about aligning your heart with God's truth so fully that anxiety loses its authority over you. The peace God planted in you these last nine weeks will continue to grow as you practice it, protect it, and choose it daily.

Let this reflection be your reminder:
God has equipped you for peace.
God has strengthened your spirit.
God has renewed your mind.
God has healed your heart.
You are living unanxious — and this is only the beginning.

Sweet Sister,

Sis, you made it to the end — and I want you to feel the weight of that. You showed up. You kept going. You prayed, reflected, wrestled, questioned, healed, and allowed God to do deep work inside of you.

This study wasn't about becoming someone new — it was about remembering who you already are in Christ.

- Strong.
- Loved.
- Chosen.
- Called.
- Protected.
- Held.

If you could see the healing that has already unfolded in you... if you could hear the softness in your thoughts... if you could recognize how your spirit has grown steadier, quieter, and stronger... you'd see how far God has brought you.

And this is just the beginning.

Being unanxious doesn't mean you'll never face fear again. It means when fear comes, it no longer gets to define you. It no longer gets to make your decisions. It no longer gets to silence your voice or steal your peace.

You are a woman who knows how to stand firmly on God's Word. A woman who can call out lies and speak truth. A woman who recognizes God's presence even in uncertainty. A woman who knows she is never alone — even in the quiet battles.

As you step forward, keep practicing the habits, truths, and tools you learned. Keep protecting your peace. Keep leaning into community. Keep inviting God into your day, your thoughts, your body, and your emotions.

God doesn't just want you to have peace; He wants you to live in peace. I'm so proud of you. I'm praying over you. And I'm believing God will continue what He started in your life.

If you don't currently have an active women's group at your church, we'd love to have you join The Sisterhood at missiondrivensisters.com or start a small group in your area with us at missiondrivenchurch.com. I'd love to stay connected with you and watch what God does in your life.

With love,

Bridget Irby

Continue Your Journey Toward Freedom

What you've just worked through is only one part of a bigger story.

The *You Are Not Called* series was created to help Christian women break free from the emotional struggles that quietly keep them stuck—often beneath the surface of faith, responsibility, and strength.

Each book in the series focuses on a different area where many women feel trapped, overwhelmed, or disconnected, including anger, anxiety, loneliness, fear, and shame.

While each study can be read on its own, the greatest transformation often happens when these truths are layered together over time.

If this book resonated with you, you're not alone—and you don't have to stop here.

The *You Are Not Called* Series
Continue your journey with the other studies in the series:

You Are Not Called to Be Angry
A Bible Study for Christian Women Ready to Break Free from Anger

You Are Not Called to Be Anxious
A Bible Study for Christian Women Ready to Break Free from Anxiety

You Are Not Called to Be Alone
A Bible Study for Christian Women Ready to Break Free from Loneliness

You Are Not Called to Be Afraid
A Bible Study for Christian Women Ready to Break Free from Fear

You Are Not Called to Be Ashamed
A Bible Study for Christian Women Ready to Break Free from Shame

Each book builds on the biblical truth about who you are and your calling — helping you heal deeply, renew your mind, and walk forward in the freedom God has always intended for you.

A Final Word Before You Go

You don't have to rush this process. Healing is not a race—it's a relationship.

As you continue through the series, allow God to meet you where you are, speak truth into the places that feel tender, and gently lead you forward. You are not behind. You are not broken. And you are not alone on this journey.

God has more for you—and freedom is closer than you think.

Free Resources

Hey there, superstar!

You've made it through the book, and I'm so proud of you. But let's be real - reading is just the first step. Now it's time to put all this good stuff into practice. And because I'm not about to send you out there empty-handed, I've got some awesome resources to help you on your journey.

Think of these as your anger management toolkit. They're like the Swiss Army knife of emotional growth - versatile, handy, and they might just save you in a pinch (though maybe don't try to use them to open a can or cut down a small tree).

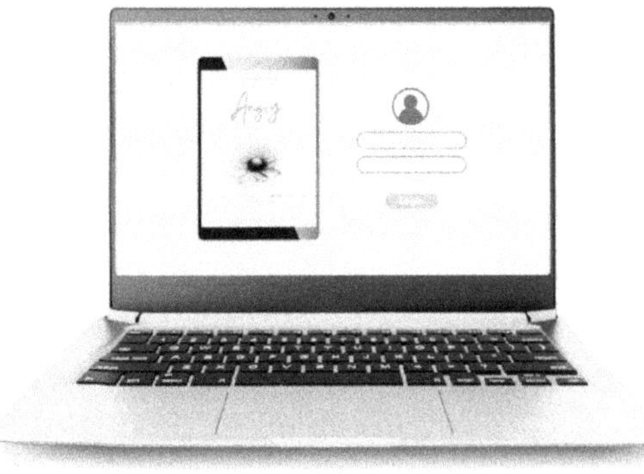

To access the resources, simply create your free account at www.youarenotcalled.com.

Inside, you'll have to the above resources plus much more!

www.ingramcontent.com/pod-product-compliance
Lightning Source LLC
Chambersburg PA
CBHW042044030726
47599CB00019B/2363